Gardening Calendar

Learn When to Plant Your Garden

Table of Contents

Introduction

You can easily grow vegetables, fruits and herbs in your own garden with the help of traditional gardening methods. To maximize the success of your gardening method, you have to focus on the right planting time, soil, fertilizer, harvest time, etc. For new gardeners, it will be difficult to find out the right time for each and every gardening activity. For your assistance, you can design a gardening calendar because it will help you to plan your planting schedule. The calendar provides information about monthly planting activities for fruits, herbs, and vegetables.

In ancient times, people follow the sun and moon for gardening because they don't have wristwatches and latest technology. The gardening calendar is derived from the old procedures and nowadays, these calendars are really helpful for new and old gardeners. You can mark your planting dates and time in the calendar and follow it to get the advantage of timely gardening. You can select vegetables, find out their plant time and prepare a calendar with accurate dates for planting and harvesting. The gardening calendar will ensure the proper growth of your garden. You can timely grow your favorite fruits and vegetables.

This book is designed for your assistance so that you can design your own garden and grow vegetables in a timely manner. This book will offer guidance for each season so that you can enjoy this habit and improve your gardening skills. This calendar will be a good choice for you to save your time and money.

Chapter 1 – Importance and Benefits of Gardening Calendar

Gardening is an astounding sort of action picked by a few people to discharge mental weariness. In addition, this system is embraced to take a break from the routine life and do something productive in the spare time. Besides, other than clear weight loses points of interest planting has been exhibited to decrease stress, lower circulatory strain, lower cholesterol, and abatement control. Research portrays that lone looking at greenery or plants can deliver changes in things as circulatory strain, heart development, muscle weight, and psyche electrical activity. Through this action plant specialists can invoke sentiments of quietness and fulfillment. Furthermore, developing a gardening calendar is far more than a vibe not too bad recreation action; it has risen as a treatment for our body and soul.

Henceforth, what is keeping you from starting your own specific garden and scene arrangement? Begin it now; plan a date-book and begin planting. Start benefiting that a yard nursery can add to your life. This is the perfect chance to find your own specific inspiration driving why you should plant.

Part of the fulfillment in organizing your own garden area is picking which seed combinations you have to create. Thusly, picking varieties that work best for your creating conditions and are extremely appropriate for your environment will end up being a solid decision while building up the porch nursery. A short time later, one have to gadget an appropriate arrangement and build up a calendar to monitor good plants in a particular season and month. Taking after focuses delineate the need of figuring a timetable for planting:

1. **Ensure smooth and appropriate working:**
   Firstly, the principal accomplishment of a timetable is the preplanned attempting to satisfy the greater part of the necessities. Everybody is very

much aware of their obligations and the time they should provide for each development. It is a direct result of the timetable that smooth, effective and viable estate is finished

2. **Prevention of wastage of time and vitality:**

Besides, the timetable shows accurately what must be done at a particular time. In a similar manner, arranges the working of a nursery worker. Thusly, this avoids wastage of time and vitality. Also, confuse and pointless repetition with that regularly happens amid exercises of planting is hence avoided.

3. **Equitable dissemination of time among different exercises:**

Thirdly, a gardeningcalendar is regularly made to give due spot, growth and emphasis to various exercises of one's life according to their relative importance and inconvenience. This guarantees the side interest of a man does not ruin its way of life or work life. Thusly, keeping up a smooth equalization among the majority of the exercises and giving them legitimate time.

4. **Enhance one's awareness of other's expectations**:

Fourthly, it makes qualities like dependability and ordinariness in a man's life by putting different obligations on them. An individual is considered in charge of the satisfaction of his/her plants. These create awareness of other's expectations in the person. Hence, schedule improvement for planting is given due significance.

5. **Creates quality of punctuality:**

Fifthly, creation of gardening calendar logbook aides in making an individual reliable. One of the vital motivations behind planting is to enhance one's physical condition. In addition, it likewise helps in discharging the mental exhaustion from one's brain. By setting up a propensity for dependability, planting schedule is clearing path for improvement.

6. **Improves personal satisfaction:**

Sixthly, by keeping up the logbook, you will have the capacity to enhance the nature of your life. The lost zest of your life will be carried back with the suspicion of development and enhancement of your greenery enclosure according to the calendar

7. A gardening calendar helps you in scheduling sowing and harvesting time of all plants and vegetables. Furthermore, you will not have to memorize all of the specific months of the vegetables and fruits you desire to plant

In this way, a planting timetable must be made while you begin cultivating as your recreation action. Not just, this system will enhance the life of the plant specialist yet will likewise make this movement a treat for him. Planting like all different pastimes expects to enhance physical and mental wellbeing. Consequently, this taught method for seeking after the action will put little strides forward towards the achievement of the sought objective.

Chapter 2 – Gardening Calendar for Summer

Gardening is a progressing procedure, and, while timing is critical, don't be overpowered by a feeling of being past the point where it is possible to plant by some discretionary date.

Summer season demands a lot of care and protection from insects, pests and the heat waves. Therefore, plants must be handled with care during this period of the year. Some of the plants that can be planted during this season are as follows:

- Beetroot
- Broccoli
- Pansies
- Snapdragons
- Dianthus
- Petunias
- Bush beans
- Beetroot
- Fuchsias
- Grapes

- Mangoes
- Apricot
- Bitter gourd
- Lady finger
- Bringle

Therefore, summer season requests a great deal of consideration and insurance from bugs and the warmth waves. Subsequently, plants must be maneuvered carefully amid this time of the year.

Gardening *calendar:*

For making a gardening calendar for summer, keep following points in your mind:

- Water your hydrangeas to ensure that the dirt is soggy
- Keep in mind that amid the hot summer days some sprouts may shrink yet will recoup when the day chills off.
- Ensure you have satisfactory mulch to keep soil dampness.
- Cut flowers for the summer action

One will be astounded how quick seeds will come up and blast with development. Try not to waver to plant seeds for cucumbers,edamame, beans, pumpkins, melons, beets, winter and summer squashes, carrots, chard and scallions. Plant warmth and sun-cherishing herbs like basil, chives, marjoram, oregano, thyme and sage with desert, keeping the seed beds very much soaked. Try not to disregard to plant some fragrant scented basil in compartments to elevate summer evening cultivating joy.

Planting later yields in summer additionally applies to flowers. Plant following flowers:

- Marigolds
- Nasturtiums
- Sunflowers
- Zinnias

- Universe

Planting calendar
Use this guide to map out what and when to plant outside in your garden.

Late April (When ground temperature is reliably 50 degrees)			Early May		Late May - Early June	
Seed		Transplant*	Seed	Transplant	Seed	Transplant
Beets	Radishes	Leeks	Beans	Broccoli	Basil	Basil
Carrots	Spinach		Early corn	Early cabbage	Brussels sprouts	Brussels sprouts
Chard	Onions (sets)**		Pumpkin	Cauliflower	Late cabbage	Eggplant
Lettuce				Parsley	Late corn	Peppers
Peas					Cucumbers	Pumpkin
Seed potatoes					Dill & Cilantro	Summer squash
					Melons	Tomatoes
					Winter squash	Tomatillos

* A transplant is a seedling with roots and leaves that was grown in a small pot from seed.
** An onion set is a small immature onion bulb, which you plant into the ground.

Journal Sentinel graphic: ZEINA MAKKY / zmakky@journalsentinel.com

Sources: Anna Thomas Bates, Megan Cain at www.creativevegetablegardener.com; UW Extension: Vegetable Cultivars and Planting Guide for Wisconsin Growers; Burpee

Along the lines of other vegetables, you'll have a glorious second round of flowers and can cut armfuls for Labor Day.

June and July are likewise great times to begin seeds for perennials and biennials to blossom next spring. Gardeners sow seeds in a secured seed overnight boardinghouse transplant seedlings in tumble to overwinter, then blossom, guaranteeing me a great spring welcoming in the patio nursery one year from now.

Regardless of the possibility that you as of now have basil, carrots, chard, squash and beans in the ground, and your plants are developing great, summer is a fine time to begin a second yield to have prepared for another bounteous harvest. Later in July and August, plant seeds for fall crops like a wide range of lettuces and mesclun mixes, spinach, radishes, kale, leeks, peas, booccoliraab, braising blend, carrots, and asian treats like gentle mustards, pakchoi and stirfry mix.

Prior in summer you should ensure that you keep seedlings watered in dry pots. Continue sowing in late summer and harvest time, a large portion of these veggies will develop outside cheerfully outside in the majority of the nation even as the climate turns colder. Any insurance you can offer will help for later sowings as harvest time goes ahead - scaled down plastic and wool passages are a simple present day other option to customary cloches. Frequently simply keeping chilly winds off your plants is all that is expected to give you a truly fruitful harvest.

If, however, you are sufficiently fortunate to have a nursery or polytunnel, don't give it a chance to stand exhaust once your midyear products are out. Consider getting on infant plants modules or open air seedbeds to transplant covert as tomatoes, peppers and cucumbers get done with trimming. In a passage/nursery you can sow servings of mixed greens and greens consistently.

Tips and techniques:

However, this season is sensitive with respect to pesticide attack. Therefore, plant must be checked regularly and thoroughly. Furthermore, water the plants frequently so that the plant is not water drained

i.   Use a complete package of lawn fertilizers. These fertilizers must fulfill the demands of nitrogen, phosphorus, sulfur, and potassium.

ii. Observe the plants and check if there is any attack of pests on your plants

iii. Apply moss repellents and use pest control to avoid damage to the plantation.

iv. Keep yourself alert to snail damage. Since snails can harm your plants.

Chapter 3 – Design Your Own Gardening Calendar for Winter

Preparing the garden to bed for the winter is for the most part a matter of tidying up and concealing. As fall advances and temperatures drop, those plants that aren't murdered by and large by ice get ready for lethargy. Get out the darkened stems and foliage of yearly blossoms and vegetables to keep the likelihood of their harboring malady pathogens and bug eggs over the winter. The cool climate is a decent time to make an icy casing, dive and box in raised beds, and make general repairs.

While it shows up as though all action in the garden has ceased, there's a ton going ahead under the solid until it turns into solid. Recently transplanted trees and bushes, divisions of perennials, and solid knobs are all developing roots, drawing on soil supplements and dampness around them. Worms and different microorganisms in the dirt are as yet preparing the natural material they're finding. Doubtlessly, the natural mulch you spread to secure the dirt amid the mid-year months has generously disintegrated. It's imperative to spread new mulch now, a thicker winter layer, to secure plants and soil over the winter months. The thought is less to keep the dirt warm as it is to keep the temperature even. Once the dirt is solidified, mulch keeps it solidified. So in the event that you have shade trees, change over the fallen leaves to mulch and utilize it all through your property.

Gardening calendar:
- This is the time of year to stop cultivating
- Cut fall-shading hydrangeas for courses of action.
- Keep on watering enough until ice.
- Leave blossoms on hydrangeas for winter interest.
- Bring compartments inside after the main ice.
- Spread the base of the hydrangea with wood chips, leaves, and so forth for winter insurance.

Following plants can be planted during the fall:

- Asparagus
- Broad beans
- Kohlrabi
- Lettuce
- Onions
- Peas
- Rhubarb
- Strawberries
- Berries
- Currants

Territorial SEED COMPANY
Winter Gardening Chart

Vegetable	May	June	July	Aug.	Sept.	Oct.	Harvest	Max Storage Time	Storage Temp	Storage Humidity	Freeze Out Temp
Arugula							Winter-Spring	1 week	34-40°F	90-95%	5-10°F
Beets							All Winter	4-5 mo	34-40°F	90-95%	15-20°F
Beans, Fava							Spring-Summer		34-40°F	Dry	10-20°F
Broccoli-Autumn Harvest			TP				Autumn	2 wks	34-40°F	90-95%	Before Severe Frost
Broccoli-Sprouting				TP			Spring	2 wks	34-40°F	90-95%	15-20°F
Brussels Sprouts - Autumn Harvest			TP				Autumn	3-5 wks	34-40°F	90-95%	After Severe Frost
Brussels Sprouts - Winter Harvest			TP				Winter	3-5 wks	34-40°F	90-95%	After Severe Frost
Cabbage - Late Summer Harvest			TP				Late Summer	3-6 wks	34-40°F	80-90%	Before Heavy Freeze
Cabbage - Autumn/Winter Harvest			TP				Autumn-Winter	5-6 wks	34-40°F	80-90%	Before Heavy Freeze
Cabbage - Winter Harvest			TP				Winter		34-40°F	80-90%	Before Heavy Freeze
Carrots							Winter-Spring	4-5 mo	34-40°F	90-95%	5°F
Cauliflower - Summer Harvest			TP				Late Summer	3-4 wks	34-40°F	90-95%	10-15°F
Cauliflower - Autumn Harvest			TP				Autumn	3-4 wks	34-40°F	90-95%	10-15°F
Cauliflower - Spring Harvest			TP				Spring	3-4 wks	34-40°F	90-95%	10-15°F
Chicory			TP				Winter	2 wks	34-40°F	90-95%	Before Heavy Freeze
Chinese Cabbage			TP				Late Fall	2-3 wks	34-40°F	90-95%	20°F
Collards				TP			Winter-Spring	1 week	33-40°F	90-95%	5-10°F
Corn Salad							Spring	1 week	35-40°F	90-95%	5°F
Fennel			TP				Autumn-Spring	2-3 wks	33-40°F	90-95%	Before Heavy Freeze
Garlic & Shallot Bulbs							Summer	5-8 mo	34-50°F	60-70%	15°F
Kale			TP				Winter-Spring	2-3 wks	34-40°F	90-95%	5-10°F
Kohlrabi			TP				Winter-Spring	2-3 wks	33-40°F	90-95%	5°F
Leeks* - Autumn Harvest		TP					Fall-Winter	6 wks	34-50°F	90-95%	5°F
Leeks* - Winter Harvest			TP				Winter-Spring	6 wks	34-50°F	90-95%	5°F
Lettuce							Fall-Winter	2 wks	33-40°F	90-95%	5-10°F
Mustard Greens							Winter	2 wks	33-40°F	90-95%	5°F
Onion - Bunching					TP		Winter-Spring	3 wks	33-40°F	90-95%	5-10°F
Onion - Overwintering & Shallots					TP		Spring-Summer	4-6 mo	55-65°F	60-70%	5-10°F
Parsley Root							Winter	8-10 wks	33-40°F	90-95%	0°F
Parsnips							Winter	4-6 mo	34-40°F	90-95%	5°F
Peas - Autumn							Fall	2 wks	33-40°F	90-95%	15°F
Peas - Overwintering							Spring	2 wks	33-40°F	90-95%	15°F
Radicchio							Fall-Winter	3-4 wks	33-40°F	90-95%	15-20°F
Radishes							Winter-Spring	2-4 wks	33-40°F	90-95%	15-20°F
Rutabagas							Winter-Spring	4-6 mo	33-40°F	90-95%	20°F
Spinach							Fall-Winter	1-2 wks	33-40°F	90-95%	5-10°F
Swiss Chard							Fall-Winter	1-2 wks	33-40°F	90-95%	5°F
Turnips							Winter-Spring	4-5 mo	34-40°F	90-95%	20°F

Sow seeds during this time period. See cultural information in the catalog.

TP Transplant: These seedlings benefit from transplanting. Move at six weeks to a permanent well-limed location.

 Covering or cloching these varieties will lengthen the harvest period.

Freeze Out Temp should be used as a general guideline only. Many factors affect when a plant will succumb to cold. Our intent is to provide a temperature at which you may want to consider when to harvest and store.

* Leeks unavailable at time of catalog printing. See website for varieties.

Tips and techniques:

The short dull days and severe climate can make the possibility of planting in winter both ugly and conceivably useless. In any case, a smidgen of winter arranging can get the garden prepared for an awesome year ahead.

- **Clean:**
  Accumulate all the instruments that you have utilized in the course of recent months and give them a decent cleaning to evacuate all the earth and rust. Utilize a gentle cleanser to sterilize pots and seed plate.
- **Check walls and alike:**
  Look at wall, sheds, entryways, and different structures for indications of shortcoming or spoil and get them repaired before the snow and high winds arrive.
- **Garden Care:**
  The garden needs somewhat of a breather over the winter months so keeping the grass out is the best thing to do. Make an exception to dispose of the huge weeds, greenery and clears out.
- **Storehouses:**
  Give sheds and nurseries a decent scour and sort out each one of those greenery enclosure instruments you cleaned before. Spruce up tables and seats also.
- **The Vegetable Garden:**
  Spread root vegetables, for example, carrots and parsnips with fifteen centimeters of straw and leaves and they can be reaped all through the winter. On the off chance that snow is conjecture spread with an old bit of floor covering.
- **Plants and Shrubs:**
  Dead-head fall blooming plants and prune summer. Moreover, blossoming bushes before the principal ices must be taken out. Brush any substantial snow from bushes and trees to avoid broken branches.
- **Manure:**

In the event that you don't as of now have a fertilizer stack or receptacle, this is as great a period as any to begin one, with all the leaves and cuttings to be discarded. For the individuals who as of now have a container, a great blend will help the treating the soil procedure along.

- **Natural life:**

  Putting out fat pieces and other sustenance won't just help nearby natural life to survive the winter however will energize winged animals, frogs, hedgehogs and so forth to stay in the greenery enclosure and they will reimburse the support a hundredfold by killing numerous patio nursery bothers in the coming year.

- **Lists:**

  There are few better approaches to spend a chilly winter's night than poring over a portion of the numerous mail request seed inventories longing for the developing season to come, and arranging your optimal greenery enclosure.

- **Cover the plants:**

  Ensuring plants shed and the nearby untamed life is vital; however bear in mind the solid plant specialist! Dressing fittingly and ensuring yourself against the rigors of winter ought to be one of your first contemplations. Look at the extensive variety of open air attire at Blacks.

Moreover, whatever one does with the bulbs in the start of fall depends upon the toughness zone and the matching profundity of the ice line in one's district. For colder environments, you'll have to jump up and store handles in a cool, faint range until danger of ice has passed. In case it's ensured to desert them in the ground through the winter, essentially ahead and reveal, confine, and replant any present handles that need upkeep.You can likewise plant new globules once the climate chills off. Basically ensure they have remarkable conditions and enough time to set up roots before the temperature drops too low. Wire bone dinner or low-nitrogen manure into the soil at the base of planting openings to really commence root advancement.

Chapter 4 – Gardening Calendar for Spring

Winter is typically a calm time in the greenhouse however soon spring arrives and you'll be gotten up to speed in the free for all of seed-sowing, developing, and sustaining your greenery enclosure as it becomes animated! Getting your garden all together early will make the spring somewhat less feverish.

Gardening calendar:

1. **Place an order for summer-flowering bulbs and seeds:**

   This is the ideal undertaking for a wet and breezy day! Summer-blossoming globules, for example, Lilies, Gladiolus and Ranunculus can be planted in early spring for a bright summer show.

2. **Clear up blossom informal lodging**

   Have a general clean up and expel leaves and different trash from your bloom outskirts, yards and lakes. You can reduce the old dead development of deciduous grasses and herbaceous perennials now, in spite of the fact that on the off chance that you'd like to be untamed life well-disposed then its best to leave the clean up until early spring. On the off chance that the dirt is workable you can burrow a five centimeters layer of natural matter, for example, all around decayed fertilizer, compost or reused green waste into unfilled greenery enclosure outskirts.

3. Clean your garden

Wash your nursery before spring arrives. Before long your garden will be home to plate of seedlings and cuttings. Get out any plant junk on the floor and situates and refine with a hot course of action of disinfectant for your garden.Ensure you purify within the glass. In addition, recollect that overwintering aggravations and disease can make due in the most diminutive specialties and cleft. Whilst you're there, wash pots and seed plate to stay away from illnesses, for instance, damping off spoiling your young plants. Ventilate your nursery well all through the accompanying couple of days so it dries out and out.

4. Sow seeds that need a more drawn out season

In spring season you can begin to sow seeds of plants which require a more drawn out developing season, following are among a few of them:

- Begonias
- Peppers
- Geraniums -Pelargoniums
- Aubergines
- Antirrhinums

Also, theyshould be developed in a warmed propagator or like guarantee great development.

5. Chase down nursery aggravations now:

Pursuing down and removing resting aggravations now can save a lot of impairment in coming spring and summer. Research the crowns of your enduring plants and you may find slugs, snails and aphid areas protecting for the winter. In the event that despite everything, you haven't cleared a pot for almost a year which was of the summer bedding then do this now and be vigilant for the white vine weevil hatchlings, which live in the manure and eat plant roots. Crush any you find and be set up to treat for vine weevils this year, utilizing parasitic nematodes or compound splashes.

6. Install water butts:

Introduce water barges in on your own garden now to gather regular precipitation. Does this help the earth as well as downpour water is useful for watering ericaceous plants, for example, Rhododendrons, Camellias, and Blueberries. At the point when introducing a water butt ensure it's situated underneath a downpipe to benefit as much as possible from the precipitation.

7. Move deciduous bushes:

If by any chance you have a severely put a deciduous bush then this is the ideal opportunity to move it whilst it's lethargic. Pick a still day to keep the roots drying out. Take a generous amount of room around the bush when uncovering it and attempt to take however much of the root ball as could reasonably be expected for the speediest foundation in its new area. At the point when planting bushes in their new position, place them at the same level they were already in the dirt, and recollect to water them in well a while later.

8. Fix wall, entryways and trellis:

Despite the way that it's frosty outside this is the ideal time of year to arrive those little positions out of the way.Any broken structures or apparatuses are best settled now so you have more opportunity to spend in the patio nursery amid spring and summer. Treat your wooden patio nursery structures with a wood additive amid dry periods.

9. Recharge the soil:

Since your dirt is likely dried out and stuffed after winter.Moreover, it is a great opportunity to include dampness. Include natural material like fertilizer or compost. You may need to test your soil to see what supplements it needs, so you give it the right blend. You may likewise need to add more manure to expand the strength of the dirt and expansion the life of your plants.

8. Plant new blooms and bushes:

Once you've gotten the greenhouse fit as a fiddle and took care of the greater part of the old plants, it's an ideal opportunity to turn your thoughtfulness regarding new plants. Some of the other recommendations for this season are as follows:

- Snapdragons
- Pansies
- Redbuds
- Peas
- Lettuce
- Arugula
- Lilacs
- Tulips

Therefore, after your spring garden is ready, now it is a great opportunity to look to the future and choose what to do with your greenhouse next. It will require some consideration so it stays brilliant and excellent all through the season. Here are some brisk tips for greenery enclosure upkeep all through whatever remains of the season:

- Mid-Spring:
    i. Consider new blossom beds.
    ii. Plant some tough annuals.
    iii. Transplant seeds.
    iv. Mulch.
- Late Spring:
    i. Deadhead and expel knobs.
    ii. Prune blossoming bushes.

Chapter 5 – Plan Your Gardening Calendar for Autumn

Fall is a decent time to get into the garden. Your soil at present contains a reasonable piece of warmth from summer before the winter downpour hits, so it's an extraordinary time to get planting. Interestingly, one can get extremely creative with the garden at this point of the year.

Gardening calendar:

In order to prepare the gardening calendar for this season, one must make sure to sow all those seeds which demand nothing else but full sun, room to grow and bright sunlight. Some of the plants that are usually grown during this season are as follows:

     i.   Brassicas

     ii.   Peas

     iii.   Lettuce

     iv.   Leeks

     v.   Onions

     vi.   Asian pears

     vii.   Date plum guava

viii.   Grapes

ix.   Pineapple

x.   Swiss chard

xi.   Turnips

However, in order to make a complete blooming garden some techniques must be kept in mind while gardening,

Tips and techniques:
Following tips and techniques must be kept in mind while preparing an autumn garden.

- **Plant fruit trees:**
  The weather during autumn season is ideal for planting fruits and vegetables. However, you should avoid overcrowding all of the other plants as well as structures including fences. This will curb the growth of these plants.
- **Addition of mulch:**
  Mulch is the best friend of your garden. This will keep the soil moist, therefore, avoiding the need of watering plants by you. Moreover, it will keep the weed concentration low.
- **Use fertilizers:**
  Preparing your lawn will guarantee that it stays green and solid consistently. Harvest time is an incredible time to treat since it secures your grass through the winter months. You ought to intend to treat twice every year for the best results.
- **Prune trees:**
  There are numerous reasons why you ought to prune your trees. It enhances the wellbeing and appearance of your trees, expels dead or biting the dust branches and it can even advance yield development in natural product trees.
- **Plant globules:**

Planting of knobs is a magnificent way to deal with adds a sprinkle of shading to the patio nursery. One would be shocked what number of different tints, sizes and sorts of knobs are accessible to be utilized. The harvest time season is perfect time of year to plant them as they will have enough time to create before they are set up to flourish in spring. Globules are genuinely easy to create notwithstanding the way that guarantees that you pick a spot with a considerable measure of sunshine.

- **Fabricate a greenery enclosure bed:**

A patio nursery bed can be a wonderful segment to have in your nursery. It is the perfect spot to create vegetables or go about as an appealing purpose of your greenhouse. Likewise ensure before you fabricate your greenery enclosure bed to consider the area in light of the fact that the levels of sun and shade will figure out which sort of plants will develop.

- **Lawn support:**

If by any chance your grass looks to some degree exhausted then this time is the perfect time to resuscitate it. Remove covering and greenery using a spring tined rake and add it to the manure heap. If you have a great deal of greenery then you may need to use a greenery killer first. In ranges that get a considerable measure of wear, (for example, ways and play territories) the dirt can get to be compacted. Enhance waste and air circulation by making profound openings with the prongs of a patio nursery fork each ten centimeters over the whole territory.

Moreover, a sandy top dressing can be brushed in thereafter, trailed by a use of harvest time grass food to set up your yard for the frosty winter months. Fall is an extraordinary time to lay new turf as well, giving it a lot of time to build up before next summer.

- **Make leaf mold:**

Leaf mold adds structure and natural matter to your soil. Most leaves from deciduous trees and bushes will spoil down to make stunning leaf manure in a few years, albeit some leaves will take longer than others.

Oak, birch, beech and hornbeam decay decently fast while sycamore, walnut, horse chestnut and sweet chestnut may take somewhat more. Destroying the leaves first will speed things up. Evergreens are best destroyed and added to the manure store as they are moderate to deteriorate.

Build a substantial receptacle out of wire cross section in a shielded spot to gather your leaves in, or if space is constrained just utilize plastic container liners with openings punch through the sides to let noticeable all around. Fill the leaf container/sacks with leaves and sprinkle with water. Tie the highest points of packs and give them a decent shake before stacking them outside of anyone's ability to see and overlooking them for a long time. On the off chance that you are utilizing a leaf container you should recall to hose the leaves at times in the event that they turn out to be excessively dry. Once the leaves achieve a brittle surface they can be spread as mulch all through your fringes.

- **Plant evergreens:**

Evergreens frame the foundation of the greenhouse, giving structure round interest, thus, the more evergreens in your patio nursery, the better it will look in winter!With warm soil and cooler conditions, harvest time is the perfect time to fill those holes in your edges.Sarcococca and Daphne will bring reflexive green leaves and delightfully fragrant blooms in the profundities of winter while whatever remains of your greenhouse is torpid. For a rich bigger bush take a stab at spring blossoming Camellias or Fatsia for its expansive engineering foliage. For a more formal look, why not put resources into some crate or yew topiary. Loniceranitida, Bay and Holly can likewise be cut into formal shapes and make astounding evergreen fences as well.

Conclusion

To put an end, this book helps you in the advancement of a gardening calendar and endless supply of the plants as indicated by their appropriate months and seasons. Similarly, in the wake of understanding this book you will set up a profound comprehension about the significance of planting schedule and how it is built up. Additionally, a profound knowledge with respect to the conditions required for any plant is likewise expounded here in this book. Above everything else, planting is more than a recreation movement in an individual's life. It has a solid impact in molding one's identity. In this manner, it requests all the more arranging and diligent work. Consequently, the aftereffects of the work put in its creation reliably pay off. Regardless, the underlying stage in developing is period of a gardening calendar. Cultivating schedule has gotten to be need of great importance in light of its various points of interest. Firstly, by making this schedule one guarantees a productive arranging and devotion towards cultivating. Besides, it helps a man in allotting productive and appropriate time among immeasurably essential tasks. Accordingly, none of the main errands of a man's life are influenced in an unfavorable way. This consequently includes train and awareness of other's expectations in life and enhances the way of life of the individual required in planting. Along these lines, if cultivating moves you and rouses you then this book is the right decision for you. Since this book will expand your viewpoint with respect to planting. In addition, this book gives data that can be utilized as a part of planting vegetables and organic products in their particular months. In this way, those why should willing make the most of their cultivating must receive the methodology recommended in here.

FREE Bonus Reminder

If you have not grabbed it yet, please go ahead and download your special bonus report *"DIY Projects. 13 Useful & Easy To Make DIY Projects To Save Money & Improve Your Home!"*
Simply Click the Button Below

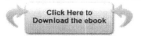

OR **Go to This Page**
http://diyhomecraft.com/free

BONUS #2: More Free Books
Do you want to receive more Free Books?

We have a mailing list where we send out our new Books when they go free on Kindle. Click on the link below to sign up for Free Book Promotions.
=> Sign Up for Free Book Promotions <=

OR Go to this URL
http://zbit.ly/1WBb1Ek

Made in United States
Troutdale, OR
08/24/2024

22281224R00018